Brides

Behaving Badly

Brides
Behaving Badly

Wild Wedding Photos
You Were Never Meant to See

BEV WEST and JASON BERGUND

WARNER BOOKS

NEW YORK   BOSTON

Copyright © 2007 by Bev West and Jason Bergund

Warner Books
Hachette Book Group USA
237 Park Avenue
New York, NY 10169
Visit our Web site at www.HachetteBookGroupUSA.com.

Printed in the United States of America

First Edition: June 2007
10 9 8 7 6 5 4 3 2 1

Warner Books and the "W" logo are trademarks of Time Warner Inc. or an affiliated company. Used under license by Hachette Book Group USA, which is not affiliated with Time Warner Inc.

Book design and text composition by Lili Schwartz

West, Beverly
  Brides behaving badly: wild wedding photos you were never meant to see / Bev West and Jason Bergund. —
1st ed.
    p. cm.
 ISBN-13: 978-0-446-69916-7
 ISBN-10: 0-446-69916-0
1. Weddings—Humor. 2. Brides—Humor. I. Bergund, Jason. II. Title.
PN6231. W37W47 2007
818'. 5402—dc22
                         2006033945

Dedication

To brides everywhere who work so tirelessly
to make our fairy tales come true,
and remind us all in the process that happily ever
after belongs to those who can hold on to their
sense of humor even when things don't go
quite as we had planned.

Acknowledgments

Thanks to all of the wonderful brides, grooms,
maids of honor, best men, bridesmaids, and
mothers and fathers of the bride for sharing their
special moments with us. Thanks, too, to the many
wonderful photographers who have contributed
their considerable talents and arresting images
to make this book so special. Thanks to the
wedding party members in our lives, most especially
Babe Scott, Aubyn Peterson, Chris Lea, and Kim Doi.

Special thanks to our editor, Rebecca Isenberg, for her
invaluable insight, tireless inspiration, and support,
and to Victoria Horn, from whom all blessings flow.

Finally, a very special thanks to Jenny Bent,
the best agent and best friend in the
whole wide world bar none.

Bev West and **Jason Bergund** are authors and newly-weds living on the Upper West Side of Manhattan. Their other books include *Pugtherapy: Finding Happiness, One Pug at a Time, Fat Daisy: Inner Beauty Secrets from a Real Dog*, and *TVtherapy*. Bev West cowrote the best-selling *Cinematherapy* series.

You're Invited...

To join us for a peek beneath the veil as gentle blushing brides turn into furious and fearless brides behaving badly whenever somebody (maybe even you) goes and does something stupid to screw up her special day.

From brides doing keg stands and topless bouquet tosses, to full-fledged marital meltdowns, our uncensored wild wedding album offers an unedited glimpse at what's lurking beneath the imported French lace. It's a reminder to every wedding guest that when it comes to the bride's special day—it's a good idea to take a deep breath, remember the love that brings you all together, hold on to your sense of humor, and then *duck!*

Come prepared to laugh, gasp, and dodge a few bridal bullets at some of the wildest weddings on earth.

And mind your manners!
RSVP
BYOB

And if you forget to send back your rsvp card . . .
RIP

BEWARE OF BRIDE

I'm gonna ask you one more time . . .
WHAT DO YOU THINK OF MY MANICURE?

See? You really can
GET A MAN WITH A GUN—
especially if it's pink

If I don't hear THE CHICKEN DANCE soon, feathers are gonna fly

No, no, nononono, NO, NOOOO! This is NOT what I ORDERED!!!!

INTRODUCING, for the very first time, the new Mr. and Mrs. Johnny Walker

Five dollars says she'll **BE TOSSING MORE** than her bouquet later

The proud
MOTHER and FATHER
OF THE BRIDE

Two of America's
MOST WANTED

CLOSED SEPT. 7
WHEN MY ONE & ONLY
DAUGHTER MARRIES
THAT SORRY, NO COUNT
WORTHLESS, SHIFTLESS
JOHN PATTERSON

Talk to the bustle, cuz the
tiara ain't listenin'

Ah, the good old days, when
MEN WERE MEN,
BRIDES WORE WHITE,
and Bacardi Silver was only $1.50 a bottle

PHOTO: STACEY TOLLACKSON

They should have said
"to have and to hold it"

REMIND ME
not to try this again sober

Now that's a
Buddhaful
BRIDE

I SAID MERLOT!

Umm, okay, I just have to say right now, this room looks **NOTHING** like a trattoria in Venice.

And where are the #(@*&#(! gondoliers?

Will somebody please **turn OFF the m&%#*%!!&ing** waterfall already?

A wedding under
a full moon
is so romantic

When you're reaching for the sky, it's best NOT to go **strapless**

BRING IT!

THIS is what you get when you meet your husband at the **SCI-FI CONVENTION**

PHOTO: URIEL DANA

Even bridesmaids
get the blues

The night of the
living bride

They're gonna redeem
them there bottles for
**A WEDDING NIGHT
AT THE SUPER 8**
once they finish the case

YOU KNOW YOU'RE AT A
redneck wedding
when the church is on wheels, the bride's smokin' a Newp, and the groom's dentistry is done in Photoshop

MR. DEMILLE,
I'm ready for my
f*&^%'n close-up

Is this a picture of:
A) a wedding
B) a prom
C) a White Snake video
D) all of the above

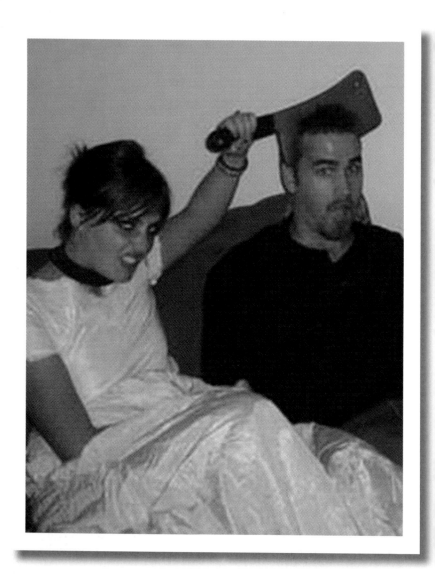

Okay, so I married an
ax murderer.
What's your problem?

What makes you think I won't cut you, too?

We really hope, for everyone's sake,
that the bride
ordered her Slyders
WITH NO ONIONS

A wedding wienie
BEFORE
the ceremony?

I got an **electric slide** for ya!

You see the faux marble
finish on that lineoleum?
THAT'S CLASS.
And the wine . . . it's imported

On our wedding day,
we should all really
find a way to finally say
"Good-bye, Kitty"

You married her, you light her

RETURN TO
SENDER

Kiss my Manolo!

Umm, I think my
GIVE A DAMN
just busted

Oh, I'm sorry, I think you've got
me confused with somebody
who gives a shit...

Are those really wedding
Ding Dongs and Ho Hos?

Is this a wedding cake, or a model for a new CONVENTION CENTER?

Marge! We need a coupl'a beers
**and a MARRIAGE
LICENSE on Lane 8**

"Ping-Pong anyone?"

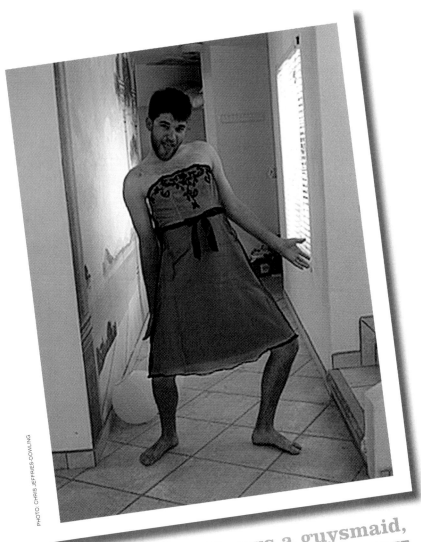

Always a guysmaid,
NEVER A GUY

Today I'm handing out
WEDDING FAVORS and
ASS WHOOPINGS,
and I'm all out of wedding favors

THANK YOU,
thank you very much and
happy birthday, Mr. President

If you aren't
talking about ME,
I'm not listening

My wedding

is better than yours, I could teach you but I'd have to charge

If you had sent in your RSVP card like I asked, I'd already know if you ordered the beef, the fish, or **the knuckle sandwich**

Yet another thing you can do with **duct tape**

Why do **YOU** have to be so pushy?

Bridin'dirty

The nickel plate on the
MUZZLE really brings
**out the radiance in
her skin, doesn't it?**

Only her wedding planner
KNOWS FOR SURE

I AM BIG,
it's the dresses that got small!

Let them
EAT CAKE

She's got spirit, yes she do,
she's got spirit, how about you?

You may NOT kiss
the bride. Or the groom.
Or the bridesmaid.

Something
BORROWED

You are STANDING on my sleeve, ASSHOLE!

Anybody got a
pair of scissors?

Plaid to the bone!

They'll always have Harry's

K-K-K-King and
Q-Q-Q-Queen
of the W-W-World!

The exorcism
of ELVIS ROSE?

This was NOT
in my job description!

It's so TACKY
to pick up the bride
on her wedding day

DOWN for the count

I'm not picking
MY NOSE,
I'm pointing at
MY BRAIN

I guess it was too late to
rent a LIMO

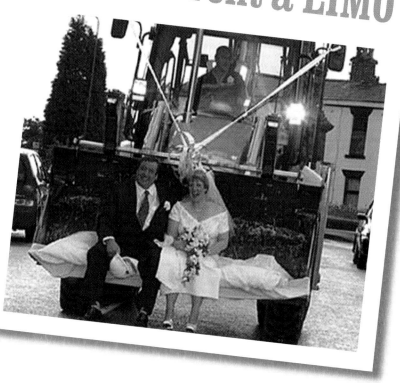

Born to bride!

PHOTO: DAVE ELTON

Obviously double coupon day at
Ye Olde Wedding Barne

I want my MTV!!!

WE'LL HAVE AN
old-fashioned
WEDDING

We hope she WAXED

Mind if I play through?

Just GET ME to

the church on time, dude!

I SAID I didn't want ANY LIP at my wedding and I MEANT IT!

This priest was ordained
by JOHN WATERS

Bride of Groucho

Where's the WOOKIE?

SHAZZAM!

It's safe to say someone
in this wedding party
is going to have really
POINTY EARS

All those cans, but the **BRIDE AND GROOM** get to drink their beer from a bottle. **That's top shelf!**

Can't touch this!

The elephant will wanna
forget this ride

PHOTO: TYRA LEGGE

Ah, I'm sick of this MUSHY LOVE STUFF, man. Wake me when the killin' starts

It's a good thing he promised

IN SICKNESS
and IN HEALTH

It's so damn **HARD**
to be a **BRIDE**

Don't step on my tan suede flip-flops?

And their first dance was the
Monster Mash

Even cakes that happen in Vegas
should stay in VEGAS

Are those the BRIDESMAIDS or the cater waiters?

PHOTO: TRACY LUNGRIN

Who GOOSED the bride?

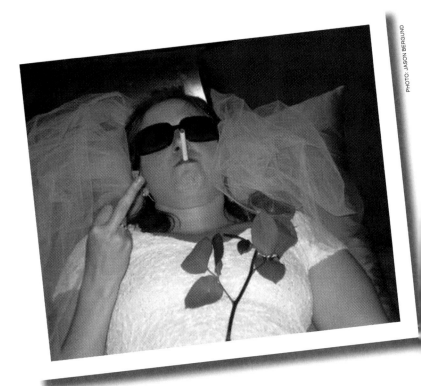

'Til death
do us part…

Just a few
prewedding jitters

WE'VE HEARD OF
doubling your pleasure,
but quadrupling it
to the 110th power?

Some grooms really
ARE DOGS

No, you're schmoopie, no, YOU'RE schmoopie!

HEY, GUYS,
that's an ice sculpture,
not a urinal mint

For all those who
SAY I DO,
this Bud's for you

Time to make the DOUGHNUTS

Grrrrrrrr baby.
VERY Grrrrr.

Now I remember where
I put those rings

PHOTO: ALBERTO GRAZI

"Yes, but was it an
ATOMIC WEDGIE?"

And if you turn her TO THE SOUTHWEST, you can pick up Showtime

PHOTO: AMRITA HUJA/ARIEL MEADOW STALLINGS

She's not afraid of VIRGINIA WOLF

PHOTO: KRISTIN FARWELL

STEP OFF,
or you get cut!

OH MY GAWD,
they did *not* just play
YMCA, again!

BAZOOMS!

GLINDA,
is that you?

This is how they
FOUND HER
the next morning

PHOTO: DANIEL HARRISON

Alien bridal party
ABDUCTION

"Can I get a WHA WHA?"

I didn't ask for the
ANAL PROBE

Best foot forward,
(WE THINK)

Watch the BOOM,
she's coming about!

Strong enough for a man, made for a BRIDE

How many bridesmaids does it take to CHANGE A TIRE?

Keep your eye on
THE BRIDE

I think we found them!

Who's your caddy?

You may now kiss the Klingon

But these *are* my
DANCING SLIPPERS

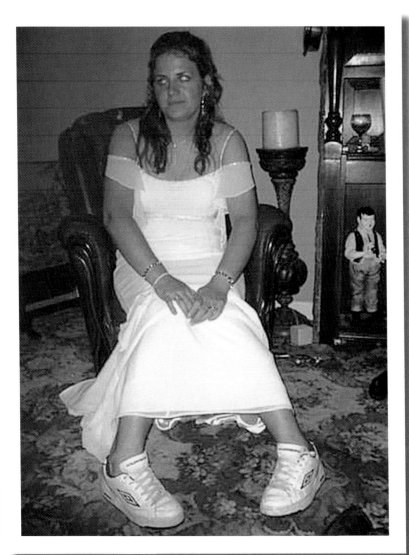

Is this a TRAIN or a new Olympic BOBSLED course?

CEREMONIAL
Running of the Brides
IN PAMPLONA

Yes, but do the drapes match the carpet?

PHOTO: ERIC SOULIERE

Say that one more time
and you will be marrying
an army of me

Well, you forgot the place cards and
your mother is on her second martini.

Things could get messy

That's one way to dress for
a shotgun wedding

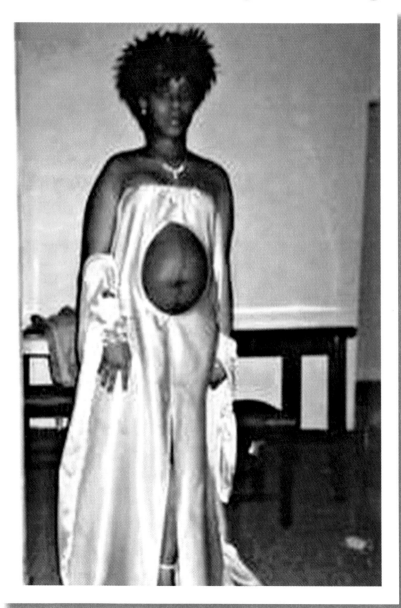

GET YOUR
motor running...

For the grand finale
they take off
THE SOCKS

If you want to know what's on a man's mind, LOOK AT HIS SHOES

THAT'S HOT!

PHOTO: URIEL DANA

SHE'S GOT LEGS,
and we hope she knows how
to use them, since there are
FOUR OF THEM

So it shall be written.
So it shall be done

What? It's HOLY WATER

PHOTO KRISTA DRAKE-LEE

Think those EXTRAS are UNION?

BARBIE'S
dream cake

Sack the BRIDE

PHOTO: MIKE ROMO

The sisterhood of the
traveling sunglasses

**A bachelorette party
in a botox office?**

Just put your lips together
AND BLOW

Does this **PLASTIC ASS** make my dress look big?

I said, maybe the DINGO ate your baby

PHOTO OLLY CLARKE

Did I just say that
OUT LOUD?

PHOTO AJ FRANKLIN

**She just got off the last
train from Clarksville**

Next I'll pull a
RABBIT
out of her sleeve

My bump, my bump, my lovely lady lump

Now sit on it and **SPIN!**

You are standing
IN MY LIGHT

Pimp my bride

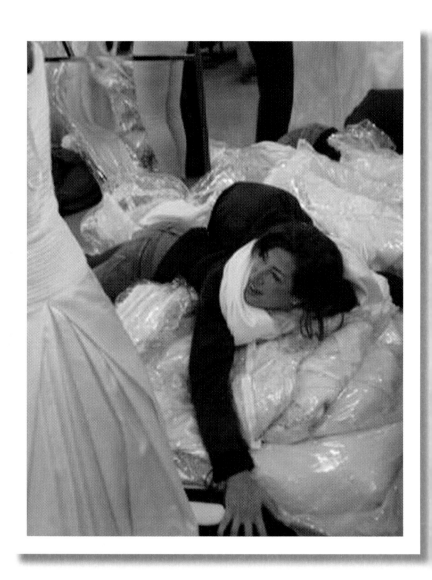

Brides off the rack

HOLLA!

Hey, the threshold's
the OTHER way!

'Til death do us
TAILGATE

BRIDE OF
Beetlejuice

Nothin' says "I DO" like a rope-light heart and a cocktail table altar. Oh yeah, and a trailer

We really hope that she isn't singing "WIND BENEATH MY WINGS," but somehow, we just know she is

"**How do you solve a problem like a BAD BRIDE?**"

PHOTO HUY NQUTEN

GNARLY

Look, a full carrot!

Is this a wedding or a RIDE at a theme park?

Bridesmaid
SMACKDOWN

It's the ever popular
WET WEDDING
GOWN CONTEST

HEY, EVERYBODY,
put your hands up

Hands off my
CORSAGE

Hey, Mrs. Tambourine,
play a song for me

PHOTO: TRACY LUNGRIN

Da-da-da-da-da-da-da
BAT BRIDE!

I am the **BRIDE** of
the DANCE, said she

I love you,
DAN BRODERICK!

GENE SIMMONS *he ain't*

The BITCH claws
are comin' out!

ADRIAN!!!!!

PHOTO: JASON BERGUND

Hold on to your bustle,
and your breath

This bride is ready to
dump on somebody

America's Next TOP BRIDE